Edward Lear's Nonsense Birds

Bodleian Library
UNIVERSITY OF OXFORD

This edition first published in 2013 by the Bodleian Library
Broad Street
Oxford OX1 3BG

www.bodleianbookshop.co.uk

ISBN 978 1 85124 261 0

Original material reproduced from the following volumes by Edward Lear:
A Book of Nonsense, 1846
Nonsense Songs, Stories, Botany and Alphabets, 1872
More Nonsense Pictures, Rhymes, Botany etc., 1872
Nonsense Songs and Stories, 1895
Queery Leary Nonsense, 1911
Edward Lear's ABC, 1914
Nonsense Botany and Nonsense Alphabets, 1927

The drawing on p. 1 is from a letter to Lord Carlingford
(Chichester Fortescue), September 1863

Every effort has been made to obtain permission to use material
which is in copyright. The publishers apologise for any omissions
and would welcome these being brought to their attention.

This edition © Bodleian Library, University of Oxford, 2013

Cover design by Dot Little
Designed and typeset in Monotype Fournier by illuminati, Grosmont
Printed and bound in China by C&C Offset Printing Co. Ltd
on 157 gsm Chinese Huaxia sun matt art

British Library Catalogue in Publishing Data
A CIP record of this publication is available from the British Library

Introduction

The parade of illustrated animals roaming through the imaginary world of Edward Lear's nonsense embodies a *joie de vivre* that has never ceased to captivate readers of all ages since they first appeared in print in 1846. The sense of ease with which these animals greet readers and their comical manner belie the virtuosity of their creator as a zoological draughtsman of the highest calibre.

Forced to work 'for bread and cheese' when his father retired, Edward Lear began to earn his living as an artist from about the time he was sixteen years old, when he produced colour plates for the later volumes of *Illustrations of British Ornithology*. Just two years later, he published the first of his *Illustrations of the Family of Psittacidae, or Parrots*, drawn mostly from life at the Zoological Gardens in Regent's Park, which immediately established his reputation and earned him a nomination as an Associate of the Linnean Society.

Observing the young Lear at work in Regent's Park, the Earl of Derby engaged him to illustrate his menagerie at Knowsley Hall. Here, after dinner, Lear used to entertain the children of the house with impromptu drawings and fabricated stories, transforming the beasts he illustrated with meticulous precision by day into works of fantasy and amusement by night.

The remarkable appeal of Lear's nonsense drawings lies in part in their ability to convey the essence of their subject with few lines. Animals—and especially birds—are endowed with individual personality, depicted with remarkable economy. This is perhaps most evident in the twenty watercolours in this book, made to teach children colours, which capture the essence of form and movement, blending ornithology and fantasy.

Lear's nonsense drawings conjure up a world where birds and people happily coexist. In this sphere, birds take on human characteristics, wearing bow ties and boots, dancing the quadrille and drinking tea. Men and women imitate birds, like the 'Old Person of Nice / Whose associates were usually Geese', depicted with long craning neck and pronounced beak. Their bodies are streamlined; they take naturally to the air, perching in trees and imitating their bird companions, like the 'Old Person of Crowle, / Who lived in the nest of an owl; / When they screamed in the nest, he screamed out with the rest'.

Lear's own self-caricature, peering out from the margins of his personal letters, is sometimes in avian guise. He presents himself, winged, in flight, or waterborne with a gaggle of geese. His exaggeratedly pronounced spectacles seem to evoke owl's eyes, a parallel noted by an observant little girl he once met in Corsica. In a letter to Lord Carlingford written on Christmas Day, 1871, Lear says wistfully, 'I think of marrying some domestic henbird and then building a nest in one of my own olive trees, where I should only descend at remote intervals during the rest of my life.'

Even in old age, when Lear's eyesight failed, the sound of birds in his garden proved a source of continued fascination. A century after his death, his love of birds, perhaps nowhere more evident than in the nonsense bird illustrations, has lost none of its appeal, drawing in new generations to the delights of this enchanting world.—S.F.

THE HISTORY OF THE SEVEN YOUNG GEESE

WHEN the Seven young Geese began to travel, they went over a large plain, on which there was but one tree, and that was a very bad one.

So four of them went up to the top of it, and looked about them, while the other three waddled up and down, and repeated poetry, and their last six lessons in Arithmetic, Geography, and Cookery.

Presently they perceived, a long way off, an object of the most interesting and obese appearance, having a perfectly round body, exactly resembling a boiled plum-pudding, with two little wings, and a beak, and three feathers growing out of his head, and only one leg.

So after a time all the Seven young Geese said to each other, 'Beyond all doubt this beast must be a Plum-pudding Flea!'

On which they incautiously began to sing aloud,

'Plum-pudding Flea,
'Plum-pudding Flea,
'Wherever you be,
'O come to our tree,
'And listen, O listen, O listen to me!'

And no sooner had they sung this verse than the Plum-pudding Flea

began to hop and skip on his one leg with the most dreadful velocity, and came straight to the tree, where he stopped and looked about him in a vacant and voluminous manner.

On which the Seven young Geese were greatly alarmed, and all of a tremble-bemble: so one of them put out his long neck and just touched him with the tip of his bill,—but no sooner had he done this than the Plum-pudding Flea skipped and hopped about more and more and higher and higher, after which he opened his mouth, and, to the great surprise and indignation of the Seven Geese, began to bark so loudly and furiously and terribly that they were totally unable to bear the noise, and by degrees every one of them suddenly tumbled down quite dead.

So that was the end of the Seven young Geese.

THE HISTORY OF THE SEVEN YOUNG OWLS

WHEN the Seven young Owls set out, they sat every now and then on the branches of old trees, and never went far at one time.

And one night when it was quite dark, they thought they heard a Mouse, but as the gas lamps were not lighted, they could not see him.

So they called out, 'Is that a mouse?'

On which a Mouse answered, 'Squeaky-peeky-weeky, yes it is.'

And immediately all the young Owls threw themselves off the tree, meaning to alight on the ground; but they did not perceive that there was a large well below them, into which they all fell superficially, and were every one of them drowned in less than half a minute.

So that was the end of the Seven young Owls.

THE HISTORY OF THE SEVEN YOUNG STORKS

WHEN the Seven young Storks set out, they walked or flew for fourteen weeks in a straight line, and for six weeks more in a crooked one; and after that they ran as hard as they could for one hundred and eight miles: and after that they stood still and made a himmeltanious chatter-clatter-blattery noise with their bills.

About the same time they perceived a large Frog, spotted with green, and with a sky-blue stripe under each ear.

So being hungry, they immediately flew at him, and were going to divide him into seven pieces, when they began to quarrel as to which of his legs should be taken off first. One said this, and another said that, and while they were all quarrelling the Frog hopped away. And when they saw that he was gone, they began to
chatter-clatter,
blatter-platter,
patter-blatter,
matter-clatter,
flatter-quatter,
more violently than ever.

And after they had fought for a week they pecked each other all to little pieces, so that at last nothing was left of any of them except their bills.

And that was the end of the Seven young Storks.

THE HISTORY OF THE SEVEN YOUNG PARROTS

THE Seven young Parrots had not gone far, when they saw a tree with a single Cherry on it, which the oldest Parrot picked instantly, but the other six being extremely hungry, tried to get it also. On which all the Seven began to fight, and they

scuffled,

and huffled,

and ruffled,

and shuffled,

and puffled,

and muffled,

and buffled,

and duffled,

and fluffled,

and guffled,

and bruffled,

and screamed, and shrieked, and squealed, and squeaked, and clawed, and snapped, and bit, and bumped, and thumped, and dumped, and flumped each other, till they were all torn into little bits, and at last there was nothing left to record this painful incident, except the Cherry and seven small green feathers.

And that was the vicious and voluble end of the Seven young Parrots.

Chewton.
Sept 5. 1872..
Edw Lear

Psittacus
Pollywobble..

One evening after dinner when on a visit to Lady Waldegrave and Lord Carlingford
at Chewton Priory, Lear drew the above parrot, a species of bird with which he
was well acquainted, having illustrated the bird section of Lord Derby's 'Knowsley
Menagerie'.

The Spectacled Owl
or the Lear ned nonsensical jargon Bird

After he had finished it Ward Braham, Lady Waldegrave's brother, drew the
caricature of bird and artist reproduced above, which amused Lear greatly.

Cockatooca Superba

Mrs. Blue Dickey-bird, who went out a-walking with her six chickey birds: she carried a parasol and wore a bonnet of green silk.

The first little chickey bird had daisies growing out of his head, and wore boots because of the dirt.

The second little chickey bird wore a hat, for fear it should rain.

The third little chickey bird carred a jug of water.

The fourth little chickey bird carried a muff, to keep her wings warm.

The fifth little chickey bird was round as a ball.

And the sixth little chickey bird walked on his head, to save his feet.

The light Red Bird.

The Scroobious Bird.

The Black Bird.

The Dark Blue Bird

The Gray Bird.

The Runcible Bird.

The Purple Bird

The Pink Bird.

The Light Green Bird.

The White Bird

The Lilac Bird,

The Brown Bird.

The Spotty Bird.

The Stripy Bird.

The Light Blue Bird.

The Dark Green Bird

The Orange Coloured Bird

The Crimson Bird.

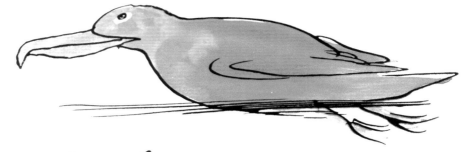

The Dark Red Bird.

The Yellow Bird

There was a Young Lady whose bonnet

Came untied when the birds sate upon it;

But she said, 'I don't care! All the birds in the air

Are welcome to sit on my bonnet!'

There was an Old Man of Dundee,
Who frequented the top of a tree;
When disturbed by the crows, he abruptly arose,
And exclaimed, 'I'll return to Dundee.'

There was an Old Man of Whitehaven,
Who danced a quadrille with a Raven;
But they said—'It's absurd, to encourage this bird!'
So they smashed that Old Man of Whitehaven.

There was an Old Man who said, 'Hush!
I perceive a young bird in this bush!'
When they said—'Is it small?' he replied—'Not at all!
It is four times as big as the bush!'

There was an Old Man with an owl,
Who continued to bother and howl;
He sate on a rail, and imbibed bitter ale,
Which refreshed that Old Man and his owl.

There was an Old Man, on whose nose,

Most birds of the air could repose;

But they all flew away, at the closing of day,

Which relieved that Old Man and his nose.

There was an Old Lady of France,
Who taught little ducklings to dance;
When she said, 'Tick-a-tack!'—they only said, 'Quack!'
Which grieved that Old Lady of France.

There was an Old Person of Cannes,
Who purchased three fowls and a fan;
Those she placed on a stool, and to make them feel cool
She constantly fanned them at Cannes.

There was an Old Person of Hove,
Who frequented the depths of a grove;
Where he studied his books, with the wrens and the rooks,
That tranquil Old Person of Hove.

There was an Old Man of Dunluce,

Who went out to sea on a goose:

When he'd gone out a mile, he observ'd with a smile,

'It is time to return to Dunluce.'

There was an Old Man of El Hums,
Who lived upon nothing but crumbs,
Which he picked off the ground, with the other birds round,
In the roads and the lanes of El Hums.

There was an Old Man of Dumbree,
Who taught little owls to drink tea;
For he said, 'To eat mice, is not proper or nice,'
That amiable Man of Dumbree.

There was an Old Man of Dumblane,
Who greatly resembled a crane;
But they said,—'Is it wrong, since your legs are so long,
To request you won't stay in Dumblane?'

There was an Old Person of Crowle,
Who lived in the nest of an owl;
When they screamed in the nest, he screamed out
    with the rest,
That depressing Old Person of Crowle.

There was an Old Person in gray,
Whose feelings were tinged with dismay;
She purchased two parrots, and fed them with carrots,
Which pleased that Old Person in gray.

There was an Old Person of Nice,
Whose associates were usually Geese.
They walked out together, in all sorts of weather,
That affable Person of Nice!

There was an Old Man of Dunrose;
A parrot seized hold of his nose.
When he grew melancholy, they said, 'His name's Polly,'
Which soothed that Old Man of Dunrose.

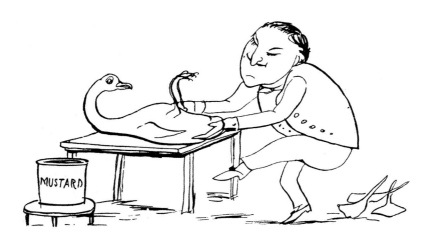

There was an Old Person of Florence,
Who held mutton chops in abhorrence;
He purchased a Bustard, and fried him in Mustard,
Which choked that Old Person of Florence.

The Dolomphious Duck,
who caught Spotted Frogs for her dinner
with a Runcible Spoon.

The Goodnatured Grey Gull,
who carried the Old Owl, and his Crimson Carpet-bag,
across the river, because he could not swim.

The Hasty Higgeldipiggledy Hen,
who went to market in a Blue Bonnet and Shawl,
and bought a Fish for her Supper.

The Judicious Jubilant Jay,
who did up her Back Hair every morning with a
    Wreath of Roses
Three feathers, and a Gold Pin.

The Perpendicular Purple Polly,
who read the Newspaper and ate Parsnip Pie
with his Spectacles.

The Queer Querulous Quail,
who smoked a Pipe of tobacco on the top of
a Tin Tea-kettle.

The Rural Runcible Raven,
who wore a White Wig and flew away
with the Carpet Broom.

The Visibly Vicious Vulture,
who wrote some Verses to a Veal-cutlet in a
Volume bound in Vellum.

D was a dove
Who lived in a wood
With such pretty soft wings,
And so gentle and good.
     d!
Dear little Dove!

D was a duck
With spots on his back
Who lived in the water
And always said, quack!
　　　d!
Dear little Duck!

E was an eagle,
Who sate on the rocks
And looked down on the fields
And the far away flocks
    e!
Beautiful Eagle!

G was once a little goose,

    Goosy

    Moosy

    Boosey

    Goosey

    Waddly-woosy

Little Goose!

H was once a little hen,
  Henny
  Chenny
  Tenny
  Henny
  Eggsy-any
Little Hen?

H was a Heron
Who stood in a Stream,
The length of his Neck
And his Legs was extreme!

    h!

 Long-legged Heron!

J was a jack-daw
Who hopped up and down
In the principal street
Of a neighbouring town.
        j!
All through the town!

K was a Kingfisher,
Quickly he flew,
So bright and so pretty
Green, Purple, and Blue.
      k!
Kingfisher, blue!

O was an Owl
Who made a loud howl,
All the night long –
A dismal old song –
o!
Poor little owl!

P was a polly
All red blue and green,
The most beautiful polly
That ever was seen.
p!
Poor little Polly!

Q was a quail,
With a very short tail
And he fed upon corn
In the evening and morn.
q!
Quaint little Quail.

T was once a little thrush,
    Thrushy!
    Hushy!
    Bushy!
    Thrushy!
Flitty – Flushy –
Little Thrush!